Flickering Lights

Ron Browning

Flickering Lights

Flickering Lights
ISBN 978 1 74027 709 9
Copyright © Ron Browning 2011

First published 2011
Reprinted 2012, 2017

GINNINDERRA PRESS
PO Box 3461 Port Adelaide 5015
www.ginninderrapress.com.au

Contents

Foreword	7
Introduction	9

1 Displaced in their own Land — 13

Survival	15
His Field	16
The Nightmare	17
Hunted Hounded…	18
Child Resilience	20
Victims Confront the World	21
Hurters	22
Teacher's Lament	23
Rafting For Education	24
Secret Suppliers	26
Mother Salween	27
Damn the Dam	28

2 Existing in a Refugee Camp — 29

Curled Up	31
Bridge in the Camp	32
Rice Shared	33
Mum, Can I Go?	34
Dance and Madonna	35
Cries Within	37
Two Portraits	38
The Abbot on the Hill	40
Flickering Lights	41

3 Resettled in a Western Country — 45

Dishevelled Here as There	47
Sound So Deep	48

Nature Connection	50
Men At Song	51
Her Wrinkled Forehead	52
Missionary?	53
Plaza Pounding	54
Twenty Years Old and Education	55
My Community Work	56
Minibus?	57
Women Weaving	58

Foreword

After Myanmar was tragically hit by Cyclone Nargis in 2009, I had the extraordinary privilege to be among the people of that country. So much of the land was devastated, so many lives and homes had been destroyed, and yet the beauty and dignity of the people shone brightly. This is a nation that has known terrible suffering, but where the strength of community and a deep spirituality remain powerful forces. This is what has inspired the work Ron Browning is presenting to us here, and I thank him for this gift.

Tim Costello
CEO, World Vision Australia

Introduction

'Flickering Lights' is the name of the one of the poems in this book. It begins by depicting a teenager in a refugee camp sitting outside his family hut on a hill. It is night and he looks down and ponders the lights emanating from the oil lamps in the huts below – a sea of lights flickering, occasionally bright and then dim, but always enduring.

The poems focus on the Karen people of Burma, on their strength and dignity, and their enduring hope for freedom. It may well be that much in these poems will resonate with other refugee situations.

For twelve years I have been closely associated with the Karen people, travelling often to the Thai–Burma border where, since 1984, 140,000 people have been forced to live in refugee camps. With the wave of resettlement between 2005 and 2008 of Karen refugees to Western countries, Australia received a few thousand through government programs. Now my time includes working with the Karen community in Melbourne.

The struggle for human rights and democracy by the Karen people, and the other ethnic groups in Burma, is relatively unknown. Yet next to the Palestinian incarceration the camps along Thai–Burma border (just inside Thailand) constitute the second oldest refugee situation in the world.

The tactics of the Burmese regime are cruel. In Karen State (East Burma) villages continue to be burnt down, children and adults are forced to be porters for its army, people are murdered and women are raped. However, through years of oppression the Karen continue to maintain a brave, defensive war.

I have written the poems in three sections. The first is about the many Karen people inside Burma who are forced to leave their villages and try to survive as internally displaced, remaining inside Burma. There are between 350,000 and 500,000 such people. They maintain their 'lights' in various and amazing ways in nearly impossible circumstances.

The second and third sections are about the situation in refugee camps and resettled life in a Western country.

The total present-day numbers of refugees around the world is estimated at 14 million with 20–25 million internally displaced in their own countries. Unquestionably, this century will see increasing numbers seeking shelter and new countries in which to live, whether due to conflicts or the increasing number of environmental disasters.

In the West we need to encounter the strength and dignity of displaced peoples and not just see them as a 'problem'. The deep cultural background of the Karen includes their traditions of dance and song, their profound sense of community, and the wondrous quality of quiet determination in their struggle amidst enormous suffering and loss. These qualities can be seen in other national or ethnic groups as well.

My aim in these poems is to be simple and direct in style. I have frequently depicted life scenes that provide an opportunity to enter the lives of refugee people and at the same time see what they can offer us. Much refugee wisdom, inner strength, humour and hopefulness, even through dark and violent moments of despair, has motivated me to write what follows.

I am not Karen but have found myself immersed in this community for a significant period of time. The poems are therefore my perceptions. I include a few that describe my own responses and personal stirrings with regard to what I have seen and heard. And a couple of other poems indicate the responses of individuals who have accompanied me to the Thai–Burma Border.

Throughout these pages I have concentrated on themes about the character of one particular refugee people. Home means the same thing for all people. It is always precious. For refugees, their homes – the homes from which they have been displaced – always stand in the back of their minds, like a shadow cast over what they do and say, wherever they are…with the continuing hope, for many, that one day they will return – home. Some years ago I came across the following poem by an Iraqi poet, Sai Farhen:

> Homes don't travel
> people hang onto their homes
> like snails to their shells.
>
> When people have to leave
> their homes, there remains a
> scar at the very place where
> people and walls meet so closely.

The quotations by Solzhenitsyn at the start of each section are from his book *The Gulag Archipelago: 1918–1956*. The drawings that accompany some of the poems have been done by a young Karen artist, Tha Do Lah.

1

Displaced in their own Land

Each year, more and more people are displaced from their villages and land in Karen State (East Burma). Some escape to the border refugee camps. Many are herded into 'relocation camps', usually a central village with gutted villages nearby. Others try to survive in jungle hideouts. All are known as IDPs – internally displaced persons.

> When we neither punish nor reproach evildoers,
> we are not simply protecting their trivial old age,
> we are thereby ripping the foundations of justice
> from beneath new generations.
>
> Aleksandr Solzhenitsyn

Survival

Violence has been in my life since
                            I was born.
I don't know anything different
                            I survive.

Will moving to the next village
                            be safer?
we ask, discussing through the night
                            we survive.

As l turn to hear your near death's
                            door story
may I listen with care so that
                            you survive.

His Field

Displaced two years before
herded to a relocation camp
forbidden return to his village
but…

To return to the village he must
because it is home
to return to the field he must
because there is rice
ready for harvest.

He knows of the land mines placed in the field
a month ago or two
he knows yet he is determined to go.

Will he become
a one-legged husband, a dead father
or provide food for his family?
– to his field he must go.

The Nightmare

It was early morning
as Eh Htoo watched the mist ascend
sitting at the door of her hut
holding her young son so tightly.

She had dreamt that night that he was taken
taken away suddenly as a child soldier
plucked
torn away.

Terror, terror, in and around
terror is now in her heart
the image in her mind strikes
her whole body as tortured
– a mother's pain.

(In 2009, 70,000 child soldiers were used by the Burmese military.)

Hunted Hounded...

Beneath mountains in a valley
her village
next to a stream
a peaceful scene?
again up and fleeing
trembling at the sound of enemy gun fire
hunted hounded hurry

Like lightening she flings her child
to her back
knots the *longhi*
making her secure
no noise, no screaming
trembling at the sound of enemy gun fire
hunted hounded hurry

Food, what of some rice?
to carry
how many days away?
pot under arm
searching to find a place
beneath leaf and vine
hearing shots and cries
hunted hounded hiding

Like this she has to flee
not tarry
and with no time to find
her older child
in the stream at play
beneath leaf and vine
hearing shots and cries
hunted hounded hiding

Now she sits panting
no pining
for her dear husband
soldier killed on duty
some months before
I must cover my child
she must not die
hunted hounded – hit?

How close, the enemy?
not knowing
she must stay, linger
mountains of fear
valley of grief
I must cover my child
she must not die
hunted hounded – hit?

Child Resilience

The resilience of the children
so incredible to see
their loving eyes
carry us
as they bear the pain.

Victims Confront the World

'Torture victims confront the world's
loneliness
mercilessness
nothingness.'

So the quotation goes
of a refugee counsellor.

Her words appear to be distilled
moving to an essence:
trauma's truth displays
the core of the world's erring
hidden from many a point of view.

Hurters

Hurters often seek
to be better hurters
they get on a roll
sadly
tragically
for them
cruelty becomes commonplace.

Teacher's Lament

It is unsafe here now
we left the village with our children
family first, the heart insists.

Deep in forest thoughts
stand my other children
crying, trying
but also wide-eyed and keen.

The students will wake in the village
'no lessons today'
when shall I see them again
to open the doors of knowledge for which they long?

Rafting For Education

Nineteen ninety-seven
the young adult group formed
Karen visionaries.

Schools were deserted that year
teachers were scarce
families relocated
pushed, prodded at gunpoint
into designated villages
crowded in.

The feisty group will find a way –
education in relocation.

Too risky to organise among the people
watched by the enemy
so in fervent whispers
they plan and deliver nearby
from an acquired raft –
the river becomes their home.

A mooring here and there
 eating, sleeping, housed
and then the odd night arrives of
glistening, flashing across the water
searchlight on bamboo
military on the prowl.

Finding, training new teachers
determined they move
upstream, downstream.

Nineteen ninety-seven
is many years ago
their work bravely continues
as they struggle and flow.

Secret Suppliers

Beneath foliage by the roadside
armed enemy metres away
a volunteer team well prepared
made a border crossing that day.

Medic, soldier, pastor, helper
these Karen folk make up the team
bearing skills and supplies
having trekked past hills and stream.

At night without torches
stealthily stealing their way
crouched, stuck, still
no doubt searched for as prey.

In their thoughts remembering
needy villagers to find
fled, bereft in the jungle
they are their very own kind.

Hoping the enemy will move on
(image of many war years)
stationary the whole week long
fixed, determined without tears.

Picturing the IDPs
sick, hungry, young and old
not far off, clustered, hiding
the team must still be bold.

Patiently now waiting
feeling delivery is secured
as the soldier looks so brave
a rare confidence has matured.

Mother Salween*

Grand and mighty   your waters flow
through the region   life to bestow.

Walking I spied   from near hilltop
scene unfolded   my heart to stop.

Rapids tumbling   brown stream rolling
awesome delight   sense extolling.

Slopes embrace you   green to the edge
large rocks adorn   children on ledge.

I waited years   to befriend you
picture once shown   flood-flush blue.

Basin you make   livelihood plenty
your pools nourish   food for family.

Bonds with nature   to those who know
trusted, you give   much by your flow.

*

Greed-monster strikes   scheming high walls
How can this be?   a darkness falls.

Plan, arm to arm   resist, secure
the precious life   of ages pure.

Down descending   I bow and sip
your waters, O Salween, wide lip.

---

*The Salween and Mekong rivers form the two great arteries of South East Asia. Many Karen villages live beside the banks of the Salween as it winds its way through Burma. Plans by the Junta are underway to dam parts of the river.

Damn the Dam

Disbelief of the people
news – the Junta will flood
their villages and valleys
land and livelihood
heritage and hope.

Information came via
emergency food helpers
information came as
shock and disbelief.

Who decides the life
of our people in this place?
Who decides any plan
that surely must be ours?

A massive dam
a massive plan
destructive of villages
great offense to us all.

Thousands of thousands
to be pushed away
loading grief upon grief
far beyond dismay.
But let us see –
Shock can lead to
our own protest and plan
                        damn the dam
                        damn the plan!

2

Existing in a Refugee Camp

These poems are based on many visits to the largest of the camps on the Thai–Burma border, Mae La, 55,000 refugees. With resettlement schemes to Western countries operating in recent years, some families have chosen to leave. When they do, other families arrive in the camp from inside Burma. Life remains much the same but the people have become more packed together like sardines. The diet is a monthly allocation of rice and fish paste. The Karen people are 70% Buddhist, 25% Christian and 5% Animist.

> The simple step of a courageous individual is not to take part in the lie. 'One word of truth outweighs the world.'
>
> Aleksandr Solzhenitsyn

Curled Up

In the camp permitted by the authorities
one day only
a day filled with sights seen and stories told.

I passed by and saw a father watching his children play
proud but with sad eyes as he sat at the front of his hut
one leg dangling over the edge, no other leg.

I heard a nineteen-year-old boy's story
so keen to learn
fleeing, he walked hundreds of miles from North Burma
to find schooling in the camp
nightmares of attack constantly haunt him.

An old woman recounts many personal tales
of her sick husband, killed sons and lost daughter
she says with a frail whisper
as faint as the still warm air around
'I can only live one day at a time.'

Loss and lament couched in the veil
of cultural restraint
suffering piled
offered without tears.

Inner tears I take back to the town
a night and a day thereafter
my lump limp body,
curled up, foetal-like
comatose from feeling a little of the weight
the load that they carry
their crippling heavy load.

Bridge in the Camp

The bridge to her friend's house
is a joy to cross.

Back from school, the same walk
there each day
same lessons, same day, same…

Homeward, a thought, an inner smile:
the bridge, and arriving at her house
she drinks some water and goes –

To the bridge, the feeling again…
'walking to see my friend'
crossing over she feels uplifted
amidst another ordinary day.

Camp confinement
downward spiralling
to perpetual boredom…
and yet, making do
finding her way
a moment, a feeling, a bridge.

Rice Shared

Every Sunday
some mothers bring rice
to their beloved church.

Every Monday
the good grain is taken
to hungry families.

Every other day
all the homes check supplies
first to feed their own.

And come Saturday
these mothers plan to give
again to those wanting.

Mum, Can I Go?

Saiah nags her mother
an impulse takes charge of her
to go, yes, go into Burma –
forbidden for any refugee.

Now she is a teenager –
a trip, let's take a chance!
no, then a resigned yes
her mother worn permits
with a friend taking off
to find her auntie.

But soon the inevitable –
a Thai soldier confronts them
an aggro *Yut, pai nai?**
is lashing in her ear.

With little fear she sweetens him
with a nice question engages him
(soft heart even of a soldier)
released, to her aunt she goes.

Now some years later
dramatising her story,
Saiah is alive
with pride and humour
symbol of emancipation.

*Stop, where are you going?

Dance and Madonna

Open-mouthed, open-air dance
the Aussie student sat –
she watched –
gesturing high into the air
jumping and bending low
forty young dancers powerfully moving
spreading, covering
the dusty sports ground
in a harmony of motion
a drum beating
an old trumpet rattling
exuberance personified, communalised
culture and passion are one.

The dance ended
with the thrill still in her ears
she turned her eye
at the side-ground to spy
drawn to, drawn in
(even though filled with the splendour displayed)
to a woman in the dirt
her own age, slumped
bare-topped, shriven shoulders, bent
a puny child in her arms
hungrily
desperately nuzzling
wrenching her dried-up breasts.

Her eyes fixed on the mother and child
from the thrill of the dance tumbling
the student's spirit crashed
striking rocks of despair
contrast, shock occasioned
of dance and Madonna.

Cries Within

I cannot but let it all touch
                     my life
now surfacing but not yet clear
with emotions of yesteryear.

Their cries well up within me
                     rising
I cannot turn away this time
a mountain of justice to climb.

The discords of innocent suffering
                   find me
they trigger, stir, summons and spin
vulnerable strains appear within.

Then I see inside that a fire is lit
                     deep down
concern and outrage aflame
may these never retire or be tame.

Two Portraits

Suffering produces endurance, endurance patience, patience character and character hope. (Romans 5:3)

I had met both men before on this border
of sustained survival and struggle
but this time each became iconed in my mind.

William enters the room
anchored, low-eyed
in some solid holding
although not an elderly man–
he is possessed of
memories of those oppressed
transcending generations:
he remembers…

His countenance is steady
strong in weakness ever
beholding as though in meditation.

He had studied abroad, various disciplines,
determined to train for the people's service;
looking, his eyes could be misunderstood
as blank, empty, obtuse…

*

Many are acquainted with Simon's wise ways,
pastor, teacher, conciliator
loved, voluntary refugee
staying, he sits and ponders
again I feel in awe of him
realising that to be
in his silence is encounter.

Slowly words emerge –
recollections rarely heard
of sacrifice, of miracle
rendered with a warmth extended
historical moments relived –
pain and promise –
in the presence of a man
whom you know knows:
an embodiment of the people
alert from lengthened years in his bond
with the Suffering One.

The Abbot on the Hill

The monastery stands
firmly
in the middle of the camp
narrow and long.

The monastery welcomes
children
and all wanting space
in their confinement.

As foreigners we visited
interested
to see the monks
and their devotion.

As foreigners then invited
to ascend
to the hut and pagoda
on a nearby hill.

The abbot there sat
smiling
inviting us to stay
to pause and ponder.

The abbot then spoke
knowingly
of the youth and their uncertain
future, calmly.

Flickering Lights

At night from the high spot
of his hut and home
in quiet
he often sat on a rock
and gazed at the camp scene
the flickering of oil lamps
shining from under thatched roofs
casting around shadows.

He was a young refugee
not knowing any other life
many years in the camp
surrounded by barbed wire
enduring with his family.

The climb to carry the rice
each month was tiring
up the hills, along the path
returning to his hut and home.

Rice and fish-paste diet
scarcely avoiding malnutrition
he panted, puffing
fatigue, mingled with anger
at the conditions, the years,
the caging, crushing opportunity
from war years raging.

Yet at night from the high spot
of his hut and home
in quiet
he often sat on a rock
and gazed at the camp scene
the flickering of oil lamps
shining from under thatched roofs
casting around shadows.

Strangely he found himself smiling
almost a vision of what might be –
beauty!
portraying gentleness and peace
can freedom come from this imprisonment?
in time can a new life emerge?

The view brought him pleasure
making space in the mind
allowing a pride, a harmony
of his people, 'my people'
whose tune played ever in his heart.

*

I met this boy then
and later again
settling in a third country
in a refugee group
storytelling, meeting people
conveying song and sound.

One visit he was returning over a city bridge
it was night
and with flickering lights below and around
(the spread of urban sprawl)
again making space in the mind.

Images of circumstance
similar and contrasting
gave rise to wonder
and touched despair
but always, ever finding
an inner light of hope.

Did he on the bridge, that city night
see himself again sitting on the rock
outside his hut, overlooking the camp
past lights beaming
contented moment
a promise of peace
yet to come into being?

3

Resettled in a Western Country

Between 2005 and 2008 many Karen people resettled to Western countries including Australia. Families made the decision to resettle mainly for the purpose of their children's education.

> Own only what you can always carry with you:
> know languages, know countries, know people.
> Let your memory be your travel bag.
>
> Aleksandr Solzhenitsyn

Dishevelled Here as There

He appears via the kitchen
in a friend's house
back door entry
suburban
quietly, not intruding.

Grey in countenance
bearing the structures of stress and war
he was the same in the camp
not hopeless, never
but dishevelled here as there.

He carries, maintains
the burden and the days
of a people dispersed worldwide
his demeanour, inner, outer
remains unchanged.

Sound So Deep

In front of an Australian group
seemingly unafraid
a young singer stood
making melody
a rootedness in his history
unmistaken.

The composition of his song
was his very own
sound and tune woven together
and the people looked overwhelmed.

Despair was touched as he
attended
compassion held as he
crescended
conveying a stillness
centred.

Yet not comprehending
on the level of their minds
(the words sung in his language)
their hearts soared and then
to an abyss fell
impact of high and low
due to his awakening call.

The key to receiving
the gift of his song
was some place
in his being and body
offered freely to all.

A resonance manifested
urgent
by his face clearly steady
towards us and beyond
intent on a future
and present to present pain.

Sound almost straining
through him flowed
deeper tones are mingled
with an accustomed voice
from grit and gut arose.

Nature Connection

Several men in cars leave
the city
some now have their licence
to drive
never before have they been
enveloped
in this foreign countryside.

Tall buildings fade into the background
fields spread, open and inviting
they point and exclaim:
horse
sheep – many
in Burma we only have one cow!

Instantly immersed in nature
their hearts leap green
delight
a strong connection
echoing somewhere
in the recesses of their minds
fields of the homeland.

Men At Song

The men stand up to sing
their hearers watch and see
on their faces
amidst their harmonies
the ravages of war
the past caging of their spirits
marked in memory.

Her Wrinkled Forehead

'How are you today?'
again I see her worried look
intense, not hidden.

Wrinkled forehead
headaches again
her leading role
loads her with
too much to think about
too much to do.

A deep faith in her heart
and close to her family
each day is given over
to the resettled women
firmly planted in her mind
myriads, many

to unite and encourage…
together stepping forward
together stepping back.

She stood there musing
quietly
strong within
'and you know I'm homesick again.'

Missionary?

She declares
'I want to be a missionary
in my homeland'
her eyes are longing
this life to transcend
alien and compromising.

Return or rescue?
which is her wanting thought?
back to her struggling people
to rescue herself or them?
salvation summons
something calls.

Still young
schooling steady
continuing
envisioning both bright and dim
eyes lit with soft love
and questioning.

Plaza Pounding

They wandered in the shopping mall
looking and languishing
in threes and fours
older boys together
falling out
in their minds
from school where
they find standards too high
homework maze
mess in the mind.

Better to go out into this other world
lights of living
seeming success
mobile calls
keeping in touch
local connections.

And other connections they hold
with refugee camp friends
(now they also have phones)
although the threads now strain.

Unexpected domain
this third country life
tomorrow who knows?
licence, driving and a little drink on the side
pulsating, a pounding of hearts.

Twenty Years Old and Education

Education…
so hard to grasp
is this why I am here in this new country?
my mind wanders
disordered, confused
how to choose a course, a job?

My head inside is like soup
stirred
at times I am back in the camp
which way forward?
when will the stirrings stop?

And hullo community and
family expectations.

I think I need
patience in my heart
…for education.

My Community Work

I am becoming
immersed so much
in this community
        focus –
have detachment
in and through all the concerns.

Minibus?

In Australia three years and no minibus
so many youth in the community, quiet but visible
gather for weekly song and connection to overcome their isolation.

A spark, a new idea – to act on
let's visit the local car dealer
he'll understand and help our cause
seeing in the streets these resident arrivals.

I said to a young leader
come as you are from your farm job
come in your work clothes
and your muddy Blundstones, that's fine.

We arrived at reception
'the boss will be back soon, please wait'
and later
'sorry, delayed but here is the Community Relations Manager.'

Blank face at request and explanation
bland uncertainty about any help
'we'll contact you'
but they never did…
I remember the muddy Blundstones.

Women Weaving

In her middle years
she teaches community women well
weaving together at their looms
thread through their fingers
pushing the wooden bars to and fro
in this third country
connecting with homeland thoughts
lingering, blending contented memories
horrors of night and day fade
as colours merge.

Over there sits an older woman, mother of ten
working her loom with her black-tooth smile
(betel nut from the local Burmese shop)
helps her along the way
inward, to a past pleasant day.

www.ingramcontent.com/pod-product-compliance
Lightning Source LLC
LaVergne TN
LVHW021737060526
838200LV00052B/3319